The Shrieking Garden

COVER ART:
SOURGIRRRL

CURATION, EDITING & PRINT DESIGN BY:
CHAD FJERSTAD

PUBLISHED BY:

WWW.EPHEMEROLNIGHTTERRORS.COM

contents

Breastfeeding

by Jenni Zeller

A Zuko Glow

by Chad Fjerstad

"I don't wanna go," I shouted, "I'm old enough now. I can take care of myself!"

My mother had made up her mind.

"Just one more summer," she said.

I was eleven and I'd just finished my final year of elementary school.

"You'll be fine," she said, "It's Denny's brother, Dave, and you love Denny. I'm sure you'll love Dave too."

Throughout the school year, my 9-year-old sister Nikki and I would spend a couple of hours in the after school day care program, until our mom was off work and able to pick us up. My favorite of the caregivers was a guy named Denny French.

Denny had a slick black hairdo, always shining subtly by way of tastefully applied product, with a bit of a curled mullet thing going on in the back. He had bright blue eyes, straight white teeth, a warm smile, and always made me feel like he was a genuine friend. When Denny was around, I was happy to be there.

I'd heard about Denny's brother, Dave, but hadn't met him yet. He ran a local dance studio called Dance Dance Dave's which some of the girls in my sister's grade attended. Nikki had considered signing up for one of his courses, but hadn't bit the bullet just yet.

I was a little put off the first time we came down the stairs into Dave's basement. The walls were made of large concrete blocks, painted with a semi-glossy coating of midnight blue. There were only a couple small windows on one side of the room, half-buried in dirt from the outside, no taller than a foot and a half each. It was a major departure from the brightly lit day care environment we were used to.

Dave looked quite a bit like Denny, but more bloated. When he leaned down to introduce himself, his smile was crooked. While shaking his hand, I looked into his eyes and immediately felt disrupted. His eyes were the same color as Denny's, but the welcoming radiance was absent. It didn't feel right.

I met Dave's tall, bearded partner in caregiving, who didn't even make an attempt to be friendly. His calloused brashness gave me such bad vibes that my brain scrubbed his name out of my long term memory. Let's just call him Rusty.

Then, there was the rest of the litter. 6 out of the 8 were toddlers between the ages of 2 and 5. Leona and Alexandra were the only others close to us in age, each of them one of Dave's most cherished dancers. Alex was in my sister's grade and looked a lot like her, with wavy blonde hair and a gap between her two front teeth.

Leona was ten years old with red hair and a Beatles-esque haircut. She looked like a boy to me. I attempted to spark up a conversation with her, considering she was the closest to my age. She kept her head tilted down, replied with one-word responses, and stubbornly refused to return my smiles no matter how intently I joked with her.

A couple hours after we were dropped off, Dave and Rusty sat everyone down in the living room and popped a Grease VHS into the VCR. It was my first time seeing the movie. My mother had always spoken of it with incessant praise, which seemed to be the general consensus. Though I already hated the song "Summer Nights" from it's frequent radio play in the early 90's (due to the heavily circulated 1991 "Grease Megamix"), I didn't know quite what to expect from the film.

By the time we had come close to the halfway mark, I felt dead set on my opinion: I despised the movie. I hated it even more than the song. Grease was one of my earliest introductions to the psychic demon known as anxiety. Through the second half, I was entirely restless, likely kicking and scoffing obnoxiously, but I made a considerate effort not to complain verbally.

Though it wasn't enough to salvage the viewing experience as a whole, the one redeeming value was in John Travolta as Danny Zuko. Zuko was an exhilirating character; the bad boy with a kind heart who, through his charm, had enough persuasion power to get most folks jumping off bridges. Perhaps the most prominent element of that charm was his staggering good looks. Those crystal blue's had the potential to incapacitate. Even as a wee boychild I could see this.

A recent memory crept in. Denny had mentioned Danny Zuko in the past,

"You've seen Grease, right? My whole life, people've always told me I remind them of Danny Zuko. That hair, those crystal blues, and such a charmer. You've got that glow, Denny. The same glow as Danny Zuko. People love you."

I smiled, admiring Denny's "glow" and the idea of his universal popularity. I didn't doubt it. I felt it, and feeling is generally a greater truth than anything.

"But I'm not the only one, you know," he said, "You've got that glow too. That Zuko glow. You and me. We're the special ones, bud."

When the credits began to roll, I felt a great weight lifted. Ten more minutes of that and I would have shrieked. The remainder of the afternoon yielded no great obstacles, aside from an unprecedented boredom. I leaned into Nikki to discuss,

"That was the worst movie I have ever seen," I said.

"I liked it," she said.

"I hate it here."

"Why?" she said, "I like it."

She turned away to continue discussion with Alex, going over her plans to get into dance, just as she was before I interrupted her.

The next day, Grease began again. I made it about 1/3 of the way through before I began verbalizing my distaste,

"Are you really gonna make us watch this entire movie again? Two days in a row? I don't like this movie."

"Sorry, but, everyone else here likes it," said Rusty, "So, you're gonna have to watch it too."

"But, it's annoying," I said, "I hate the songs. They're horrible."

"Would you like to sit in time-out?"

"Uhhh, no," I replied.

"Then, watch the movie."

For the next hour, I sat with my arms crossed, the frumpiest frown plastered to my face, but no matter how upset I was, I resisted the urge to complain any further.

When Grease began again, the third day in a row, I could no longer contain my opposition.

"You can't be serious," I said, "Can we please watch a different movie?"

"We love Grease here," said Dave, "It's our little tradition to watch it every day."

"Every day?" I said, "No way. I can't. I'll go psycho!"

"We talked about this," said Rusty, "If you don't want to watch it, you can go sit in time-out."

"I don't want to sit in time-out *or* watch Grease! Both sound like torture. There are tons of awesome movies out there – can't we watch anything else? Literally anything?"

"Alright, get in the corner," said Rusty, with his finger pointing to the darkest corner of the basement.

I looked to Dave, "Seriously?"

"Go on," said Dave.

I was commanded to sit "Indian style", facing the corner, which was dark enough that it appeared a deep black rather than midnight blue. In the past, I'd been confined to my own room as a means of punishment, but never had I felt the sheer imprisonment I felt in that corner. Alone in the dim, my aversion towards Dave's entire operation increased immensely.

An hour or so later, the men in charge made it apparent it was lunchtime. Rusty spoke to me,

"Are you going to be joining us for lunch?"

"Can I?" I asked.

"Well, that depends," he said, "Are you ready to

appreciate Grease yet?"

"What? No."

"Well, then you're not getting any lunch."

I tried to hold back, but couldn't. I started crying. After a minute or so, Dave approached me in the corner,

"Just pretend like you like Grease, and come watch it with the rest of us."

"Why do I have to pretend? I don't wanna lie and I don't wanna watch that movie. I just want food."

"Just say you like Grease then. It's not that hard."

"No! I don't like Grease! I hate Grease!"

Dave served the rest of the kids lunch while I was left in the shadows with nothing.

Writhing in frustration, I began thinking about Denny. I missed his presence intensely. How could Dave be so different from his brother? Why didn't he have the Zuko glow as well? There was something wrong with Dave, something I could sense was missing from his eyes, but I didn't know what it was.

The kind of thoughts I generally had, concerning subjects like Super Nintendo, 311, or Chris Farley, became outmoded at the behest of an overwhelming swarm of rage-centric revenge plots. Though none of these plots may have made any logical sense from an adult perspective, the authentic desire for control became all that I knew. The only thing that mattered was finding a way to gain power over the bastards, but I couldn't figure out how. If I'd believed in God, I would have been praying.

The time spent in that corner was so draining that it began to feel like it was my entire existence. It was bad enough that the whole lot of us never left the darkness of that basement, but it was ten times bleaker in the corner. When I'd return home for evenings, I'd melt into a lump and pout until bedtime, dreading my inevitable return the following day.

For weeks, every day was nearly identical. I starved in the shadows while everyone else nonchalantly indulged in their daily Grease viewing, while consuming their sandwiches, fruit slices, cookies, and juice boxes. Somehow, everyone in the room remained uneffected by my clear display of misery, which had basically become a ritual. On occasion, I'd catch a glimpse of some sort of concern in Leona's eyes, but every time I'd look at her, she'd skittishly jerk her head away.

Leona always sat at the foldout table with Dave and Rusty. She always wore a fuzzy purple sweater, and she never smiled. Dave and Rusty treated her differently than everyone else. They didn't talk to her like a child. They talked to her the way they talked to each other.

Three weeks deep and I was starting to feel defeated in a way that I had never experienced before. My whole body felt heavier, like it had caught some sort of plague. Suddenly, I was conscious of the insignificance of my physical body – I was only flesh and bones, a bag of meat. There was a sort of magic I'd always had that I could feel escaping me.

At the end of the day, I tried to confide in my sister again,

"I want to run away," I said, "I don't want to come back here. Ever."

"Why don't you just shut up and watch Grease with the rest of us, ya idiot? It's awesome."

I dropped my head into my hands and let out a deep sigh.

"We're going to Dance Dance Dave's tomorrow when mom gets off work, to sign me up for dance," said Nikki, "I'm really excited."

I understood what it meant to her. I understood that I would not find the solace I seeked in her, but it was not her fault - she was too naïve.

When the end of the following afternoon arrived, Mom scooped us up and we headed to Dance Dance Dave's. Dave had left the basement early that day, just after Grease finished, presumably to prepare for our arrival at the studio. We parked just outside of the front door, next to Dave's grey Camry, the only other car in the lot. Sunset had just begun, casting an orange glow over everything.

I decided to stay in the car, listening to alternative radio, while Mom and Nikki went in to complete the registration. As the last minute of Beck's "Where It's At" came to a close, I heard Nikki scream at the top of her lungs. I waited a beat, and when the screaming didn't stop, I shut off the car, yanked the keys from the ignition, and stormed into the studio.

Beyond the foyer, through the doorway to the main rehearsal room, stood Nikki and my mother. They were turned away from me. Mom was holding onto Nikki, trying to cover her eyes, as Nikki screamed, cried, and jerked her body around.

Suddenly, Nikki broke free from my mother, and

came stampeding towards me. I had never seen her look so terrified. Her face was beat red, tears streaming. As she plowed into me, I thought she was going to start squeezing me, but she carried on right past me. Not out the door, but into the corner next to it. The screaming did not let up.

Shocked and confused, I began hastily towards my mother. As I approached her, I could see something on the ground behind her. I could sense that she was preparing to stop me. She grabbed my bicep as I grew near her but I immediately overpowered her, swerving past her.

The long wall in front of me was covered in poorly-done paintings of Disney characters: Beauty & The Beast and The Lion King to the left, Aladdin and The Little Mermaid to the right. In the middle, a caricature style rendition of the most prominent characters from Grease, with Sandy and Danny front and center, of course. Between the paintings and I, there was a body.

Dave lie in a pool of dark red blood, in the center of the dance studio. A bullet hole was visible just above his left eye while a handgun sat an inch from his hand. The golden orange rays of the setting sun shined through the studio's floor-to-ceiling windows, spotlighting his lifeless cadaver.

My mom grabbed me again, this time pulling me towards the exit.

We spent the following day with our aunt.

In the car on the way home, Mom started to say something but got choked up. A tear streamed down her cheek. Once she was able to speak, she informed us that

Dave had been accused of molesting Leona. After taking a moment to process the news, her and I agreed that if he killed himself, he was probably guilty. Mom's single tear developed into a base level cry, which triggered a domino effect, causing Nikki to start bawling.

As my family wept beside me, I felt the darkness of it all coursing through me, but also a rush of relief and a strange sort of validation.

Dave's eyes came into my vision again. They had been drilled into my mind since the first time I peered into them. I thought about the absence in them, which I no longer perceived as an absence but rather a drab color I was previously unable to comprehend. It was the same color as the basement corner.

Part One:
Pertaining To LaBanna's Journey Into Understanding SENTIENT CEMENT

by LaBanna Babalon

Somewhere in the Deep South, visiting relatives from a judgmental estranged family, I relived my death from a past life. I was already a very sexual being, scolded constantly for my awareness of the ancient art of seduction. Late in the night I decided to lock myself in a room. I completely disassociated. I came back to being surrounded by a group of worried adults and a distraught baby sitter. Apparently I tried to kill myself by asphyxiation.

Ten years later, twenty years old, wide eyed in New York City, I learned the manner of the aforementioned trauma.

I was on my way to meet my best friend Anna Kate while she nannied in a park overlooking New Jersey. As I was walking on Hester Street towards the Hudson River bank, I crossed paths with a neon sign reading: $10 PALM READING. With only 100 odd dollars to my name, I felt an urgency to enter. The clairvoyant was a Romanian woman in her 40's with a window area in the front. Some crystals, two chairs, and a small table rested between us. She told me it was necessary to do a tarot reading, and I obliged, telling her I didn't have much money. She said she would work with me. She felt an evil energy associated with me and asked if I was ever sexually abused. I could not recollect any memories other than typical child's exploration and curiosity of the human form. She said she needed me to give her my mother and father's birth information, as well as my own, and to come back in thirty minutes. Upon returning, I don't remember much other than her telling me she could do an exorcism for me and pour precious metals into a pyramid representing my energetic body to rid me of this entity. I told her the money I had given her was all I had to my name. She asked if I would be willing to baby sit her children in exchange. We agreed to the exchange and she had me meet her family in the room behind us. There was a large wrap-around couch with dozens of children and adults watching a big screen TV. She gave me her number and wished me luck. I returned to the water's edge and found my friend Anna Kate who had grown worried about me. It had apparently been hours and I didn't recall much of what happened. She was concerned that I'd been swindled. A few months later I realized how much she'd helped me.

In the near future I visited Philadelphia on a Chinatown bus with my new Piscean friend Camissa. Meeting up with her friend April at a warehouse party, we all decided to split a quarter bag of mushrooms with another girl I'd never met named Cecelia. The night took a turn and I decided to sleep at Cecelia's house as April and Camissa were entertaining an annoying boy I had no interest in being around while tripping. It was a nice night, so we decided to walk to her house in South Philly. The houses are gorgeous old Victorian mansions with huge flower gardens. We danced almost all the way home communing with flower devas and fairies blessing us with their luminosity. We approached a very old house with a huge sun room, but all the windows had been tinted dark so you couldn't see into them, only out. Something was magnetically pulling me towards the home when Cecelia grabbed my hand and screamed

"SARAH NO!!!" in the voice of a very young child. In that moment a gargoyle demon made of ash came rushing out of the house. It created a portal of fear to trick me from running away from into it. Without Cecelia's hand reaching out and grabbing mine, I think I could have been lost forever in the fear portal. She had no idea I had any other name than LaBanna. Sarah was my first name which I hadn't gone by in years.

We both were rightfully freaked at this point and ran across the street into the neutral ground, then continued walking back to her apartment. All of these memories came rushing back to me. I remembered the psychic taking me to the astral plane where only our chairs and the table with the tarot cards remained, in a field of limitless low sitting fog. She told me that in my past life I had choked myself to death by hanging alongside my sister, commiting mutual suicide. She also told me that I'd run into the entity who embodied my father in that life, who had been torturing me and a group of women for eons. In this life, she informed, we could dismantle the patriarchal raping beast for good. Cecelia recalled earlier that day, a piece of automatic writing written slanted in a pyramid. It was a detailed first-hand account of sexual and physical abuse ending in self impaling by a fence. Cecelia got spooked and asked if we could refrain from discussing until we reached her home, where she would feel safe. We walked in silence the rest of the way, contemplating this shared hallucination.

We made some tea and took a deep breath, finding our

voices again once inside. It wasn't long after Cecelia read the poem out loud that a ghastly fist punched through the ceiling made of the same disembodied ash from before. I stood up and screamed, recalling what the psychic told me, that in this life we could kill the raping beast.

We took a bath to ease our spirits and remembered all these details from our past life, which soon became evident The Virgin Suicides was based on. It was a true story, that neither of us had seen since we were teenagers. I did not realize all the sisters were being sexually abused. The psychic told me that no one believed us, even our own mother, so, to end the heinous atrocities we banned together in a suicide pact.

I was reminded to revisit this memory while steaming with my friend Nadia at an athletic club from the 30's in New Orleans. We were admiring all the marble surrounding us when a woman came in who Nadia immediately recognized as the actress who played the character Cecelia in the film. Cecelia was the youngest daughter who was impaled on an iron fence. I had no idea this was her name in the movie. We moved to the dry cedar steam room where I told Nadia the story, explaining the woman's relevance.

Hollywood is often a ritual. Shared hallucinations are real, and I know now how to effectively rid the earth of these particular demons. If you feel a calling to do this same kind of work, please reach out to me. You do not have to be a woman to participate for we've embodied many sexes through the eons. Holding space for this type of healing is so greatly appreciated and I thank everyone who is actively repairing their DNA for the shit that will be going down soon. My mother visited a shaman in Australia who told her the cycle of rape would end with our line and I truly believe it will. I lost my virginity being date raped at 14.

The Rules of Repression

by Kris Kidd

Memories revisit you while you are in the shower, trying to rinse the weight of the day off your shoulders. They make that difficult. Almost impossible.

You turn to your reflection for guidance, but you don't recognize it.

You can't ignore your depressive thoughts, so you give into them.

You sink deeper.

You spend the majority of your free time texting a blocked number.

You continue to take responsibility for a tragedy that had nothing to do with you.

Lingering out in the waiting room before leaving your therapist's office, you watch as she finishes jotting down notes on your latest session through a small crack in the door and you resent her for it. The concept of getting better sounds like climbing Mount Everest. You've defeated yourself just by admitting it. Now you'll never be likeable enough to be a protagonist. Literally who gives a shit.

You prefer to be angry. It's easier.

You find little to no pleasure in being comforted by others.

THE SHRIEKING GARDEN

You get anxious when asking for things like emotional support or whatever.

You feel like you're missing something, but you're not sure what it is yet.

You wander away from hope because you've got no fucking clue what to do with it.

Drunkenly calling up suicide hotlines is somewhat of a hobby of yours even though you know for a fact that you'll never have the balls to go through with it. You've apologized to the operators so frequently for taking up their time and energy that they've begun immediately reconnecting you to a whole other hotline entirely, forwarding all of your calls over to a different group of professionals who are contractually obligated to care about your melodramatic nonsense.

You hate the way the words "I'm sorry" always seem to fit.

You have difficulty trusting people who tell you they have no regrets. How is that even possible.

You drink black coffee and chain-smoke cigarettes because having all-white teeth is racist.

You enjoy being in control of the specific ways in which you choose to lose control.

You eat six frozen meatballs a day: three for breakfast and three more for dinner.

They come in zip-locked freezer bags of 24. The bags cost $9.99. Your food allowance is roughly $20 a week. The rational part of your brain is aware that this isn't healthy. The rest of your brain is telling that part to go fuck itself. Running from your problems can be a pretty great form of cardio. Calorie counting is kind of like magic.

You are competing against a clock that only you can see.

You don't have much time left.

You know your body's a temple, but you've never been very religious.

You keep telling yourself that all of this is actually happening to somebody else.

You rarely fall for your own bullshit.

Perusing the aisles of grocery stores late at night has become a means of self-punishment. Grapes are half off tonight because they're in season. Cashiers and bag boys are staring at you like you're some sort of a crazy person. Their stares make sense to you because you are a crazy person.

You wonder what's wrong with you, but then you remember.

You Googled 'Post Traumatic Stress Disorder' a couple months ago and a whole lot made sense.

You never could take "no" for an answer.

You have always despised rules and authority figures.

You seek out the attention of any and all men to fill voids left behind by one in particular.

This one time, when you were in the first grade, your teacher caught you touching yourself "inappropriately" during an arithmetic lesson and then she reprimanded you in front of the entire class and you were very embarrassed. You've never forgiven her for that and you still, to this day, have trouble doing basic math.

You can't think of many things in this world you're more afraid of than being abandoned.

You have mastered the art of the preemptive strike.

You remind yourself that it's impossible to lose if you don't try. So, why bother.

You always leave first now.

You disappear before anybody else get a chance to.

Meanwhile, you're still bounding through life, propelled

by the chaos theory. The past informing your future. The muffled feedback of memory, hazy and distorted by the passage of time, perpetually predicting your inevitable downfall. All because an adult made you an adult when you were just a kid. All because some man wanted you in ways you weren't ready for and disposed of your childhood when you needed it most.

You hold onto that hurt because it's all you have left of him.

You wonder if doing that makes you "part of the cycle."

You no longer believe in stuff like fate or coincidence. What in the hell is a happy accident.

You used to think your scars and bruises might eventually turn into lessons.

You wound up disfigured and you're still totally uncertain.

Sliding down to the bathroom floor slowly, you hug your knees to your chest and wait for the drugs you just ate to kick in. After a while, you start begging. The word "please" becomes a prayer. That prayer goes unanswered. 'Typical,' you think to yourself. The pointlessness of all of this washes over you like a revelation. If history could be reversed, you'd definitely go back and change some things, emerge a better person.

You don't care if it all falls apart in the end because as far as you're concerned it all already has.

You just wish that you could be mad at somebody different.

You would like to move on to a new kind of hatred and be sad about something else for once.

You should probably start trying to get over stuff like that.

You don't know if you'll ever be capable of getting over stuff like that.

Lately, you've been scrolling through an app that specializes in temporary romantic connections. It divides all of its users into various different sections based on surface-level statistics like ages and body types. They have an entire category named after father figures. You're still trying to find the humor in that. You're beginning to wonder if you'll ever be able to.

You desperately want to experience an emotion that's somehow stronger than the urge to cry.

You ask creepy old guys you meet online to choke you out during sex because for some reason the sensation of oxygen deprivation still feels new and exciting every time.

You have gotten used to getting used by dudes you don't even like.

You do this shit to yourself and you do it on purpose.

You keep your pain current because you feel like you deserve it.

Guilt courses through you like an electric charge. Here you are again: a slave to your own impulses, imprisoned by your own evasive desires. On hands and knees in some stranger's apartment, embracing misery with miserable company and calling it 'freedom.' Outside, there is an entire world that will never belong to you. A distant realm of possibility and potential that was, quite simply, never in the cards for you.

Your inner child is rotting away at you.

Your heart is misfiring.

Your narcissism is no match for how much you truly hate yourself.

Your every move is fueled by regret.

Your shame follows you around everywhere like some kind of relentless stray cat.

There are people out there who genuinely believe that their lives are going to turn out okay. Isn't that crazy? A grief counselor once told you, "Honey, you don't even know what the rest of your life has in store for you yet," and you said, "Yeah. Exactly." She didn't get it.

You expected so much more than all of this.

You did the math.

You just weren't very good at it.

You really are your own worst enemy.

You made things a lot harder on yourself than they needed to be.

Anyway.

You could have been somebody.

BUT WHO ARE YOUR REAL FRIENDS?

by Krystall Schott

But

WHO

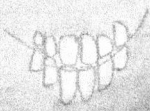

ARE
Your
REAL FRIENDS?

Shit Starter

by Allessandra Tipacti

Anytime I've ever gotten in trouble, or been made out to be a monster or a bully, I always remember my mother (or even my teachers at school) telling me that I'd never been the one to start it. In fact, I was quite friendly and lovable when shown kindness; perhaps to a fault. The trouble came from my reactions. Someone would start, then I'd respond. Once having responded, I somehow would be depicted as the monster, the bad one, in the end; my instigator completely forgotten and pardoned. I've always been treated like I was too much.

When I was 5, my family lived in Eagle Rock where I was born. That street was way different back then, still a bit sketch, still a bit violent. I somehow had this understanding that all the kids I played with were the younger siblings of something menacing (just like me). At the time, my dad (from Peru) was a cocaine dealer and my mother (from Italy) always attained a pretty pleasant demeanor. I have memories of tender moments of her– a 50's housewife misplaced in a world of chaos. My dad was either not around or causing trouble or being wonderful. Like his screaming, getting violent with us from a come-down, or buying me a Barbie in a good mood...I REALLY loved them.

A kid next door is preparing to remove his training wheels from his bicycle, just like me. He is one year younger than me and this is the reason why I am the butt of the joke. He's making my life hell. At a very young age I can still remember ME coming out and into my own thoughts saying, "It's unreasonable to be jealous, I know you want to hate him but this isn't his fault." I wanted to hate him. I had an eye out for him; like he was some kind of secret asshole. Even then, I respected that this was probably my own pride…

One quiet afternoon, I'm on the sidewalk in front our home practicing how to ride my bicycle without training wheels. I feel a THUD! on the back of my head – the little fuckface pegged me with a lemon. Taunting me, he had already figured out how to ride without the wheels. Finally, all the thoughts that I had about him, my paranoia, my inhibitions about thinking he was a little prick, all came to a boil. I calmly walked to the side of my home and picked up a PVC pipe that was on the dirt. I WHACKED him across the head and knocked him out briefly…

I felt….satisfied, and not just satisfied, it felt like the right thing to do. It was simple, like seeing a smudge in the window glass, wiping it away and walking off to tend to other tasks. I practically forgot it had happened almost instantaneously. One time an ex told me that being a kid is kind of like being on acid and I always recall this time when I think of his strange analogy.

Just like the occurrence of a dream, once happened; then the next phase….

And so, the next phase!

That night…

I'm sitting with my favorites…my parents. We are watching The Simpsons, my favorite. We hear BAM! BAM! BAM! on the door.

I literally had no idea who it could beeeeeeee…… weirrrrrrrd right?????

There. About a dozen angry, screaming Vietnamese people.

Still, I thought, "Whats going on?"

I zoom in. On the floor, with an icepack on his head, I see the crying, screaming brat just blubbering in agony…I take a moment, and think, "Ohhhh yeahhhhhhhhhhh" and feel the satisfaction within my realization.

"Did it hurt, Fuckface? Sucks having no sympathy doesn't it?"

I felt the deeper satisfaction of my work. Most definitely.

I zipped back into reality with an inescapable feeling of eyes on me. I looked up to see my dad, with his smoldering, God-like, Peruvian stare that could frighten even the bravest. He caught me. He saw my satisfaction; he saw that I fucking did it. And he was just DYING to hear my answer when he asked me, "What did you do?"

Quite frankly, he didn't need to hear my reply. I don't think I'd lied yet by this age, but I was trying to figure out how.

The angry mob is screaming louder and louder and louder…

What do they want?

I am getting really nervous and annoyed. The kid's older sister, whom I admired, threatened, "Come over here." I replied, "NO!" very aggressively. My father got more pissed off each moment.

Through the screams, he grabs me by the collar and rips me from the floor, throws me over his lap, tears off his belt and starts lashing my back and bum. I felt both the leather and the buckle. The angry crowd kept screaming, soon my screams matched theirs. In agonizing pain, my cries grew louder. When finally I look over at the kid, his cries begin to settle, and now I see his satisfaction. The same satisfaction he had at the start, when he threw that lemon at my head. Now I'm screaming the loudest.

They slowly walk away. His mom couldn't look anymore. I was beaten very bad, publicly. I was bloody and bruised.

My family and I didn't live there for much longer; but in the time before we left, I no longer had any friends to play with. All the kids on the street rejected me.

Over time, I forgot why I had even done what I did. I was just convinced that I was bad.

This story is important to me, or at least something that I think of often. In my adulthood, as a grown woman, I can't necessarily say that this story is the cause of a repeating theme, but it does repeat.

I have a strength about me that is recognized, and in that I feel a certain responsibility (and perhaps a burden) to tip-toe, and to speak cautiously, so as not to come off as a power-hungry bitch who is overtly trying to dominate every situation and person she is near. I have been expected to take tougher treatment than many others, like a dog on a choke chain. People have spoken to me very disrespectfully, and the few times I have clapped back (not physically), people have become horrified, telling me to calm down, in hopes that I won't "punch down". When have I ever had a "punch UP"? Certainly, I've never been allowed to throw back what has been dished out, even in jest.

Whether it's battling sexual harassment in the workplace or defending myself from personal assault, I am always to blame. Violence always chases me.

I've always felt sorry for myself because of this. Until this past year, I always wished someone would worry or feel sorry for me just once, or have my back.

A series of traumatic events occurred in 2017-2018. I was sexually assaulted twice, lost my job, and my best friend died. Throughout this time, until now, people speak to me with concern. Now, I am told repeatedly to stop apologizing, that it's ok to say how you feel; ask a boyfriend for space, tell someone to back off and state your boundaries. I finally became so crippled by this lonesome monster who I no longer wanted to defend. I felt driven to the other side of this spectrum, as a victim. At times, a high level of anxiety and inexplicable fear comes over me affecting my ability to have successful relationships. Somehow, the concern of others made me worry for myself far more than I ever had before.

It is not about wishing for power nor the sympathy of being a victim, its about needing space to just be. Somehow that has always been so hard to attain.

Big Death

by Hether Fortune

Red and raw. Smoke sticks to every surface and it feels like home. The cigarettes were always burning, left to think in glass corners. White tank tops and sweatpants and mumbling, always mumbling. These things live side by side. I am in a now that is parallel to a then. They never untangle, they just keep stacking. Microscopic shrapnel eroding it from the inside out. I can still see it: frame by frame, pooling lava. Bloodshot brown eyes burning holes into my stomach. It was then and it is now.

Breathing in. Breathing out. The lungs can be stretched easily, but as soon as they are released they go back to their original shape.

They are somewhere in all black. Mumbling The Lord's Prayer. Swaying in suspended reality, arms wrapped around the knees. All the roses will be thrown. The Great Mourning Mother will stay in the black forever. Somewhere she is wailing. Beating tiny, frail fists upon the massive grave. The sons gather around. Lowered heads, stale tears. They wonder at the motivations of others and the property to be exchanged. Scales begin to show. It was then and it is now. I can see it, just as I can see the page in front of me:

Sticky in a Michigan summer. Very small in the entertainment room. Video games, controllers, used plates and soiled napkins. I didn't eat it and I didn't play. I was barely there. Facing the wall, a game of Solitaire on the desktop PC. I made sure to disappear myself when I was done. I wiped down the keyboard and pushed in the chair. My shoes were always off so I could fade away softly. The dragon breathes fire. It was then and it is now. I stay undetected. Still, my face is burning. Red welts over and over again. I fold into myself like a paper crane. The distant thud of my small body echoes from the bottom of the quarry. I built myself a wall. Floating ribs.

Here there is safety. The wall of the windpipe is very strong, and elastic. My head turns from side to side with ease. Moments are reel-to-reel. They are simultaneous, the happenings. Like ghosts I pretend not to see until there is a collision. I don't scream. I just freeze, the way a mouth closes tightly when it feels the coldness of the air. I am watching it shuffle from room to room. It is looking for a fire poker. It waits for the candle wax to soften. Shaping and reshaping and stab and collapse. Dancing flames in its eyes, jumping jack flash. Pill-dusted saliva. It's too much. Waste products carried in the bloodstream, dangerous if they stay too long.

"Is the water cold enough for you, Princess?"

I want you to listen. I know it doesn't fit your narrative. This is your first Big Death but it was me in the tower. You put the corpse on a pedestal: The Making of A Martyr. You are erecting statues in its honor. Reclaiming the Truth as if it is a thread to weave. And it is. It was then and it is now. You are allowed to spin out. I am always spinning. That enormous trauma qualifies you. Scars tell stories that deepen and fade. Cut yourself again, for effect. I understand. Nobody came for me. I climbed down my own hair. Some of the water you drink is to dissolve waste.

I can't pretend I don't see it in me: the cigarettes, the candles, the red eyes, the flame. I have scales, too. It hurts because it's true. Lies are cheap and easy. That's the thing. That's it. And you know, Jamie Lee Curtis was a knockout in True Lies. The double-edged sword sees every side. Your face is that face and my face is still red.

Women and children have shorter vocal cords. The sounds they make are higher in pitch. But this is a low, guttural rumble in the distance, from the mountain. You have to hold your ear to the ground. You have to listen with your hands.

Unbur

by Phoenix Askani

dening

I would like to tell this story as accurately as I remember it, but I have omitted a few details and changed names for privacy.

"A child's life is like a piece of paper on which every person leaves a mark." -Chinese proverb

I believe I was only seven. At seven, I was taking jazz dance classes, playing in the sandbox, helping my mother plant flowers, practicing my handwriting, riding my bike, making friends - becoming my own little person with hobbies and interests. It's been over twenty years since the court case. In the years since, I've seen little girls playing outside or under my watchful babysitter's eye with a protective heart and wished through each exhale that I could protect them all. They remind me of the little girl I was, before one person changed the trajectory of my childhood. We're going to call that person Robert.

I was visiting with two relatives - we'll call them Deborah and Mary - at their home where they lived with Deborah's long-term boyfriend who we were told to regard as family. My two brothers and I would be spending the night there while my parents went out to a work-related event. This kind of sleepover was a rare occasion, but a welcomed one. At the house, there was a dog - a grey poodle, I believe. I enjoyed entertaining myself with the pup especially when my brothers played amongst themselves or denied my requests to join them in a two-player videogame. Sometime before tucking into bed that night, I recall Deborah's then-boyfriend, Robert, suggesting just the two of us wake up early before everyone else to watch our choice of cartoons as a special treat - a simple yet effective persuasion.

The next morning, I awoke to a whisper. We went down the hall into the living room just barely filling with sunlight. He flipped the TV on and we sat on the couch to watch the best morning cartoons - or so I thought. Most of this memory - the imagery and detail - has been buried away like old paperwork tucked into a file, then locked in a figurative filing cabinet in my mind. I've kept it there, spending most of my life avoiding any recollection of everything that happened from that moment on. The file is always there buried away, the acknowledgement of its existence comes and goes. You're easily reminded sometimes. You see his name on a clothing brand at the department store. You see a report about another child, just like you. Occasionally, you're caught off guard when you close your eyes and the memory passes through your mind as easily as any negative thought could. You do your best not to let it snowball. You learn coping mechanisms.

The day #MeToo flooded the internet, I sat in bed

on my laptop, toggling between depression naps and sobbing over the stories on my screen written by other survivors. The stores of women like me. I felt proud of their strength and vulnerability, but heartbroken by the masses. Was there really a woman I knew that wasn't harassed by men from a young age? My filing cabinet was now cracked open. Every memory tucked away of a time when a man violated, harassed, sexually assaulted, manipulated, or threatened me - exploding in my mind. Moments of misogyny and terror played on loop for days.

My first memory of a deplorable man began that morning, on the couch. Everyone else peacefully asleep. My parents wouldn't be returning until lunch time. I didn't expect him to touch me. I didn't expect him to ask me inappropriate questions about touching me. Couch and cartoons became police report and court case. I'm not sure I recall much detail beyond what I later told police.

An adult man molested me when I was a little girl.

It is not an easy sentence for me to say - I still almost don't believe it is real at times. It was just as real as his prison sentence. I have blocked so much of it out, but I remember the image of my legs... my little girls briefs... his hands where they did not belong, where they should have never been. I have attempted searching for the police report archives and sex offender database because I wanted to know what happened to him after he got out of prison

46

thanks to "good behavior". I called the police station it was first reported at in the suburbs of Chicago, IL, wondering the truth and hoping he was somewhere six feet under. I didn't dig deep enough to find my answers, but those answers are not currently part of my healing process.

I've seen the daunting statistics regarding child sexual abuse. I'm one of those statistics. I didn't tell anyone at first. I came to learn that it's very common for children to not tell anyone about their abuse in the first 1-5 years. I also learned most children are sexually abused by someone they know and trust.

The abuser told me not to tell. I stayed quiet, avoided him more whenever visiting or at family events. The abuser was still dating my relative, Deborah. I remember the fear of telling her the most. One day, in a shopping mall food court, I decided to tell Mary and Deborah about what had happened in their home. I told them my biggest secret over french fries and was asked not to tell anyone else. It was now our secret, just the three of us. They knew that he touched me and asked me not to tell anyone. He continued to live there and nothing much had changed, yet.

I imagine only the three of us knew for a year, but the exact timeline is a little hazy. I pushed my dark secret deep and far away. I tried to carry on with my childhood and kept myself well distracted with a plethora of indoor and outdoor activities. I was participating in recreational sports, consuming myself with books and crafts, playing with dolls and Legos or our family dogs, shooting basketball in the driveway or going to the local park's playground with my brothers. I'm grateful for the privileges my parents afforded our family, as I was able to immerse myself in so many hobbies by second and third grade, while also taking summer vacations with them in different parts of the United States each year.

The strange thing is that I remember very little of this time frame in my life after the abuse and before the "real telling" outside of what was photographed. I know what I did because it is documented and through those images, I can piece together my life. Not every adult remembers their childhood well, but several physical or psychological traumas can be responsible for memory loss. Writing from a prompt regarding something simple from an image or from a childhood memory often helps me process these unconsciously repressed parts - but not without some mental or emotional difficulty.

Eventually, I told a friend. There was a slightly older girl from down the block named Christina who was over at my house and we played games in my bedroom. I don't remember exactly what I said to her, but she knew something was wrong and I had a feeling I was right to tell her by the shock on her face. I begged her to keep my secret with me, because I was still afraid. It felt better to share it with someone and just be heard rather than be told again to stay quiet.

The truth is I don't know how much longer I stayed quiet.

It was Thanksgiving Day and I was likely about ten years old. We had plans to go celebrate with Deborah and Mary at their home. I'd recently got the news that Deborah's dog had passed recently and wouldn't be there as a source of distraction from the big scary man I knew only to avoid however I could. It was easy to keep my eyes down and speak less if I was playing fetch with a dog. The dog having grown up accustomed to a loyal German Shepherd in our household, I knew dogs made me feel safe. I was no longer safe.

My eyes filled with tears. My skin ran hot. I didn't know what to do and my body became tense. A clear feeling in my memory of hopelessness and fear stood on a day meant to be spent with family and in gratitude. I spent most Thanksgivings in my early adult years chalking up my occasional bad attitude to "the historically inaccurate and problematic holiday" and not consuming turkey, but I knew deep down that I also hated that day because all I could remember each year was how I felt then.

I opened the door to my bedroom, adjacent to my mother and father's room, and interrupted them as they chatted while getting ready for the big holiday. I had to tell them now. I needed to feel safe. I sat on the edge of their bed breaking down in tears and told the truth, watching their eyes as their hearts broke. I can only imagine how difficult it must have been to navigate those feelings as parents, finding out that your only daughter was abused by someone you thought you trusted. I'm fairly certain my father would've wanted to bury him right then and there, but that wasn't an option. My parents also learned that Deborah and Mary asked me to stay silent rather than tell them. They were distraught.

Thanksgiving was cancelled that year. I never had to see him again. A more casual dinner in place of my father's plans to carve the turkey. I felt somewhat guilty for interrupting the day for everyone else, yet so entirely relieved and protected. My mother and father gave me every ounce of their love and enveloped me in their arms. They continued to support me and protect me through every necessary retelling of the story and later begin taking me to children's therapy appointments.

The officer that handled my case was a warm, kind woman. She made it easier to say what I needed to say. I remember the papers on the desk, the fluorescent lighting and my impatience to get through with the repetitive nature of it. I wanted to be done with it. I had to speak to multiple professionals and we were preparing to take him to court. I was going to take the stand and retell the story again, only in front of Robert this time. A child, pointing out her abuser to his face as witness to the prosecution.

I must have expressed my anxious feelings clearly because the events that unfolded were like unexpected gifts. Christina had to speak to the police as well because she was one of the first witnesses to my story. We received news The State of Illinois was going to allow Christina to testify as a witness for the prosecution in my place. The State of Illinois won that case and I was so thankful to her for granting me that peace. I never had to see him again, after all. I could sleep in my bed at night knowing he was behind bars, a feeling not every survivor will know. There is not always a paved route or "right way" to justice and justice for a survivor is highly subjective.

My late great-aunt showed me grace and comfort when she gifted me a stuffed animal named "Courage" that week. She gave me a warm embrace and told me I was brave and strong. I wasn't extremely close with her because I did not see her terribly often, but she was always so loving and I never forgot this kindness she showed me. A small gesture from a very big heart.

The thing that repressing a memory over time does to you - it makes for distant memories and shapes your mind differently. I lost the sense of purity I was taught about growing up in a church. I lost the ability to trust in members of my own family. My childhood would never be the same.

It's okay not to tell your story. It's not okay to pres-sure a survivor to share their story if they choose to keep it private. It's not okay to tell someone that they cannot tell theirs. Survivors should not be silenced. I'm glad I told

Christina and my parents. I slowly felt less alone. I had felt dismissed and left with my hurt and confusion for too long.

I eventually stopped wondering why Deborah and Mary told me to remain silent. It became evident that Robert had a prior on his record that was quite similar in nature. My parents didn't know about that or I would have never been allowed near him. I never knew if Deborah knew the truth. I never knew if she was protecting him or protecting herself. I wanted to believe she had no clue about his prior, no selfish desire to diminish my trauma to avoid the inevitable upheaval. Mary came around and apologized profusely to my parents as quickly as possible, but it felt more uncomfortable with Deborah. Our big family events were uneasy for years to come - I recall even birthday parties being thrown more separately for a while. The tension was palpable. Even at a young age, I knew that I had unintentionally become the center of attention and source of drama within the family. Over time, that became less apparent. I continued the therapy, eyes focused on toys as I sorted through feelings with the doctor. I believe the incident and added fact that I held this darkness in for so long at Deborah's request lead to increased difficulty trusting people - especially men - throughout my entire life. More years of therapy ensued and mother picked up every book she could about depressed youth.

I work toward forgiveness but healing is not linear, as I remind myself daily. I forgive people so I don't have to hold the weight anymore, not for them. I never sought out to hold a grudge toward my own flesh & blood. I still see Deborah & Mary when I visit with family and I have love for them because they are my family and they had to face the darkness in themselves after their mistake was realized. I know they care about me and I know our lives were all changed.

It feels odd to say "I forgive Robert" but in a sense, I have made peace with it. I feel grateful that justice was served, something not every survivor has the opportunity to experience. Not every survivor even has the option to report or even safely identify their abuser publicly. I am grateful to my family for guiding and protecting me through the entire criminal process and to my mother for always taking the time to take me to various mental health professionals and being a stable arrow in my life.

Twenty years after the court case, I'd circled through many coping tools and settled on working through the bulk of my grief, anger, bitterness, and sadness in therapy or on the page. I can write a story from a survivor's perspective but I choose not to live in the shadow of my own victimhood. A place I was in before that I cannot go back to is one of repression and guilt for something out of my own control. I don't even want to give my abusers that much credit, but of course I've asked myself if my life would be different if events X, Y, or Z didn't occur. Does it matter? Would I have become who I am today?

I don't believe any child deserves to know trauma, deep scars sewn into the skin just as we're barely beginning to discover who we are and develop our initial physical, social, and mental skills. I should've been flipping through illustrated storybooks rather than giving a police report that evening. It's almost like I left my body the day I stopped holding it all in. I want to hug that little girl, thank her for her unburdening. I've chosen to keep the story private to a few loved ones, doctors, and at times, support groups until I felt the fear of writing this story and did it anyway.

I wish I could tell you I knew all of the answers to protecting other children from things like what happened to me. What I do know is that there are preventative measures, such as Body Safety Education, you can utilize as a parent. As an adult around children that are not your own, it is also important to give children space and never force them to hug you regardless of how cute they are.

"Body Safety Education" is a method of sexual abuse prevention education for teaching children correct names of their private parts, the difference between "safe" and "unsafe" touch, and to not keep things secret that are uncomfortable or feel bad to them. It feels devastating to assume we cannot control it when statistics say at least one in ten children will be abused before the age of 18. We can make a difference. Allow children to feel comfortable opening up to you. Allow children an understanding of their own body autonomy. If a child I know well or am even related to doesn't want a kiss or hug in that moment,

I grant them that space. Children will show affection in their own time and even family should not force physical affection. I believe children should be taught from the earliest possible age the rights they have over governing their own bodies. Children may not be able to consciousnessly consent, but they can begin to understand what consent is. We can do better for the children of the future. We have to do better.

Seventy-three percent of child victims do not tell anyone about the abuse for at least 1 year.

Forty-five percent do not tell anyone for 5 years. Some never disclose.

At least 20% of child abuse survivors are under the age of eight and never tell or do not recall the abuse.

95 percent of sexually abused children will be abused by someone they know and trust.

Power

by Krystall Schott

I'M GOING
TO SCRIBBLE
OVER
THE
WORLD

Cement Hand Prints

by Actually Huizenga

Have you ever seen the video or read about Harlow's Monkey Experiment? These baby monkeys are forced to ween from a wire structure "mother" with a bottle. Next to the 'wire mother' is a 'cotton mother' without milk. The baby immediately goes to the cotton mother after feeding- spending most of the day with it- sleeping on it, being comforted by it. Another experiment had some monkeys forced to live with just the wire mother, without the comfort of the milk-less cotton mother...these babies of the wire mesh breast soon began throwing themselves on the floor, rocking back and forth...

So, baby animals need comfort and as little abuse as possible- right? And sexual abuse is gonna be very high up there. Sexually abused children are the ones rocking back and forth- confused as to why they do not have a 'cotton mother.'

So when you ask me about my first experience of sexual molestation, I immediately feel as though I do not deserve to relate my relatively easy one. I had loving parents and so much room and support to develop my brain into the places it wanted to go. I am one of the lucky ones. I have talked with so many humans abused at sordidly early ages...that I feel almost as though I am complaining about something that I have no right to complain about. I feel that I am belittling the abuses that so many small, undeveloped humans must face. So many humans who have to fight harder to regain their own minds because they were denied a comfortable environment to sponge within.

I always want to skip through the 'childhood parts' of biographies. I read a lot of them, and those parts are definitely the most boring. Serial killers and other psycho and sociopaths have slightly more interesting childhoods because of the torture. But then, there I go again, finding joy in the sorrows of the world...

I would never wish these abuses on anyone, but I do enjoy the research. So...that is partly what this is about, right? Not just the sordid flashiness of how interesting we all are because we have all experienced abuses and rapes and the, lets be honest, normal horrors of a human existence? The bigger the brain, the bigger the capacity for Evil! Let's never forget that, humans! Chimpanzees and dolphins have nothing on us.

So let me tell you about mine. But, please excuse me if I sound like one of those assholes on cocaine so excited to share the triumph of my victimization!

One day I randomly asked my mother to take me to Grauman's Chinese theater to look at the celebrity hand and food indentations in concrete. I had seen it on TCM. I was wearing a cotton candy pink, stupid dress and frilly socks and those black shiny shoes with metal taps on the bottom- so I could tap dance and be annoying (as all children most assuredly are).

So ya- this whimsical kid of whatever age the height of a desk is... is walking down Hollywood boulevard, feeling poetic about that Los Angeles golden pink color of Christmas at dusk and getting excited about postcards on those plastic turning towers in the shitty tourist shops... I was so intrigued by those butts with neon thongs inviting the passerby (or whomever gets this postcard in the mail) to come to 'California with the Beach Bums!' Of Course! SO then we get to the Chinese theater in all it's dusty glory... an oriental princess in an elaborate white world full of khaki shorts and blocky colors and buzz cuts and dirty socks and leg hair.

In the cement, some shoes were heels and some were giant male shoes- and some were bare feet! AND Whoopi Goldberg put a few of her dreadlocks down! SO that was really great. I thought it was spaghetti or something but it doesn't matter- cuz it's Whoopi and I was a stupid kid swimming in my brain- looking out at images- deciphering social and historical root systems...I did know who Shirley Temple was- and amazingly my hands fit into hers! But I couldn't test my feet because my mom wouldn't let me take my shoes off! Shirley was apparently one of the amazing groundbreakers- putting her bare feet into the cement. Poor little rich girl indeed!

I went to go look at some others- I thought about beautiful women lying in shiny dull pink and cream satin coffins- did this one get cremated or decide to let her corpse rot in her diamonds? It always intrigued me. Especially that hole at the bottom of the skull- I knew that grave diggers always had to clean that area out because the brain chunks rattle around. Just a thought... as I sway through the khaki and jean colored flesh-masses but then BAM! A man in an army jacket and probably covered in flame tattoos (I can't be sure- maybe tribal), blockades my path with an arm swinging down and a hot, balmy mass of finger bones swathed in skin, now cupping my cotton-veiled mound of hairless genitalia. It was forceful and fast like a pigeon flying into a window, but without the innocence or sadness of that. It was all just fast enough that no one noticed, and he could pull away to sniff and lick his fingers and let me look up to his pouty, kissy smile. Some smiles are inappropriate.

Exiting The Flesh

by Vero Anease

edited by Whitney Evanson

THE SHRIEKING GARDEN

Life pulled out of the flesh

Pale.

Blue tones swept across the body
beginning with
the face
replacing any sign of life
with an appearance of death

Blood poured from the nose,
Blood poured from the mouth.

An airway, completely severed

into
two

separate
parts.

lungs eighty percent full,
filled with lake water.

THE SHRIEKING GARDEN

Injuries sustained
typical of a hanging
due to the force of being
pulled in
the water by

the rope

wrapped
around

my neck.

Approximately 1 p.m.
July 11th, 2004
is when

life
castigated
my vessel.

exiting
and
entering
the flesh.

THE SHRIEKING GARDEN

The back and forth between
lost
and
regained pulses
continued for
(at least)
fifteen minutes

There was a passing
or
transition state
In which I felt
pure confusion

It wasn't unyielding white lights
But rather,
cloudy, blurred views

My eyes (became)
suddenly aware
of
the situation

as I wondered
for a second
what I was looking at...

And that is when realization struck
all at once

THE SHRIEKING GARDEN

I knew what
it was
the surrealism
of it (all)
put me in denial
It was my body...
my flesh...
my vessel.

And I felt myself existing above everything...
detached from my flesh,
detached from my body,
detached from

everything
else
that existed

Seeing your own body
as you float above it
and watch
is...
indescribable
the feeling of it
all...
undefinable

THE SHRIEKING GARDEN

The haziness of it
felt like watching a low budget film
with the only scene
featuring my body
laying on a boat,
dying

I have absolutely no memories of the accident
(fortunately)

I experienced:
no pain,
no panicking,
and
no suffering.

I have only
that brief
and vivid
out of body experience
(my only memory of that day)

THE SHRIEKING GARDEN

I was rushed to a hospital
and once there
given amnesia inducing drugs

causing me
to forget
the details of the accident
(which it did)

in hopes of preventing PTSD
(which it didn't)

I believe that there is something else after death...

and you do not
just simply
die.

Your vessel does,
but you are not your vessel.

"Energy is neither created nor destroyed"

THE SHRIEKING GARDEN

Due to the hanging injury
I (still) suffer.
I still feel...
partial paralysis of the vocal cords

and the fragility of our vessels
is something I am reminded of
every
single
day
The silence this injury has inflicted on me;
I feel like
a mime
and this world
is
my invisible box

Violence

by Christopher Zeischegg

My friend asked if I would help him to shoot up our high school.

"Yeah," I said, even though I'd never held a gun. I thought it was a good idea.

My friend was upset because his girlfriend broke up with him right after she'd sucked another boy's dick. The other boy had high cheekbones; defined abs. He had a nice hair-cut. It wasn't fair that the other boy existed, said my friend, in so many words.

I drew a crude map of our school and marked an X near the locker room, where we planned to abduct the other boy. "We could stab him in the throat and hide him in one of the stalls," I said to my friend.

He agreed.

Already, we'd forgotten about the guns and the other people we'd sworn to murder.

***

Years later, I read one of my friend's anti-gun posts on Facebook.

He'd become political. In his words, A common-sense human being.

I 'liked' his post and sent him a FB message. Because we'd moved to different cities and no longer spoke to each other. I wanted to know what he was up to.

He messaged me back. *I'm good.* He told me about his job.

I told him that I worked in post-production, editing corporate videos.

Cool, wrote my friend.

***

I met a girl at a club. We exchanged numbers. She texted me nudes and then pictures of herself from middle school and high school.

She was younger than me, and grew up with cell phones that came equipped with cameras. She'd learned Photoshop by age twelve, and used to make Eric Harris and Dylan Klebold fan art out of her selfies. She showed me a few pieces that she'd saved to an old Flickr account.

I told her that I found the 'art' endearing while I fucked her ass, at her request.

***

The girl from the club ghosted me. Or I ghosted her. It was

hard to say for sure.

I went back to the club and exchanged numbers with another girl. She was nice. Attractive. Into charity. She spoke highly of me to her friends – before we'd gotten to know each other. We ended up dating.

We spent Thanksgiving together, dishing out soup at a homeless shelter. A few homeless men flirted with her while they stood in line for their meal. She smiled at them and complimented their clothing, which was dirty and smelled like shit.

I asked her, later, why she'd put up with the homeless men. I knew she hated catcalling; that she claimed to have pepper sprayed a guy who'd talked to her on the street.

"They're less fortunate," she said. "A lot of homeless people have mental illness. Or they grew up with abuse. Why not show them compassion?"

I told her that my parents divorced when I was young and that my father used to hit me.

She asked if I'd been molested.

I said that I wasn't sure.

"You're not sure?" She said that she'd been raped.

I said that I'd never met a girl who hadn't.

"Your mother loves you," she said. "I love you."

"I know."

We talked about the world and how it was awful.

"I don't know why," she said. "But I still want to have kids."

***

The girl and I stayed together long enough to endure another holiday. She shared her New Year's resolutions with me: to spend more time with each other, make more money, and give back to the community.

"What's a cause you believe in?" she asked.

I was caught off guard.

"Gun violence," I said, because I'd seen the news earlier that day. There'd been a school shooting. "I mean, stopping it."

"Have you thought about volunteering at Americans for Responsible Solutions? They're a non-profit that started in the wake of Sandy Hook."

***

The following week, I went to a gun range and held my first pistol. I didn't shoot anything. But I stood in front of an employee and placed the pistol's barrel in my mouth.

The employee stared at me, terrified, but like he wanted to understand; to know me. No one had ever looked at me like that.

He threatened to call the police.

I put the gun down and left. I'd never felt so alive.

A feeling

of being disconnected and mostly just pieces of a person

by Meaghan O'Keefe

Shandra

by Josh Beck

I remember when I was asked to contribute to this new literary endeavor, on the topic of childhood trauma. I instantly agreed - but at the time had no idea what I could contribute. After much internal debate & introspection I decided on the following narrative to share, which is a first hand account of my own experience & entirely factual.

I decided to write about that which I know best, & that is death & dying. I was introduced to many concepts at a particularly young age, coming from an openly queer family in Portland, Oregon. But the beauty of death is that it knows no region, no sex, race nor religion. This is a lesson many learn much later in life or after many grievous experiences - but for me this was not the case.

People always ask me if I'm an only child, & though there are two people I consider brother & sister on this earth - they are not blood. But, I am not an only child.

On July 17th, 1988; approximately 9:30 AM at Portland Adventist hospital - Shandra Loree was born. I was there, I held her at five years old, & I was so excited to be her brother.

Flash forward to Thanksgiving day. I remember that we shared a room, her crib just a few feet from my bed. I remember my mother tucking us both in the night before. But at some point my sleep was incredibly disturbed. I didn't know what it was or why, but I knew in my heart that something was wrong. I awoke & immediately ran to my sister's crib & peered in, only to find her blue, lifeless.

Although beyond my grasp at the time, I knew somehow the severity of what was happening & ran to my mother's room across the house to alert her.

My next memories are of her running to our room, screams, paramedics, tears, and confusion. The memories from this point until the funeral are a blur, & it's a miracle I can remember this much.

I remember my five year old self standing at her wake, with my tiny black suit. I remember my family, hugging & crying over this sudden & unexplainable loss - which they labeled "sudden infant death syndrome."

But most importantly I remember - even at five years old - a tremendous energy in the room when she left us & one that awoke me & drove me to alert others. I could feel her soul leaving, it filled every corner of the room & even in my infant understanding I knew the gravity.

Since that day she's visited me more than once & I'm absolutely certain of it. She's been watching over me. Thanksgiving has taken a completely different meaning to me ever since.

Particularly in moments of near death do I notice her presence more - on one instance I was in a car wreck on New Year's Day where I had an out of body experience, I couldn't see her yet I felt her presence & heard what I thought to be her voice - telling me everything was going to be ok.

I wish I could have seen the woman she was capable of becoming.

I Am The Light

by Niko Sonnberger

As a child, my safe word was "ultraviolet". My first memory was shadow play. I was bound by blackness: velvet curtains drawn, my body blindfolded, sunscreened, muting every photon, holding the darkness like a black hole. The sun was my imaginary playmate, it was the most mysterious object I would never know. I would take afternoon tea parties with my phantasmic, ten thousand lumens of death in a playroom cemented in umbrage. Two spoonfuls of sugar in a tea cup filled with solar flares. Cheers: to our cooling, black cores.

They say the sun will burn out in five billion years. If I could live that long, if I could find a way, I would be absolved of every ritualistic veil covering my small, young life. Most people fear the night: the monsters, what it hides, what you can't see, the dark fueling each nightmare. My great horror was the one symbol for life on earth: sunshine, sunbeams, sunlight. My fear was corporeal, my vessel betraying itself, aching the body, the skin engirthed in UV light, ready to sing my body into ignition. Without my cerements, sunlight hitting my skin felt like a hundred bees stinging you at once. I was always the moth, never the butterfly, always the sunset, never the sunrise.

When I was seven, I learned about nightshades. My heart swelled. I thought they were plants that could grow in the dark. Eggplants and tomatoes were eaten during every meal voraciously, ceremoniously, thinking they were like me. Of course, I unearthed the disappointment quickly and thereafter discovered bioluminescent sea creatures. I especially liked the Angler fish, which has a light attached to its head. I sympathized with the algae that shines indigo when touched. Was this who I was? Screaming neon to threaten a predator? Did I want to grow gills and live in the bowels of the ocean where the sun could not reach? I wanted to shine my body. This was me. Was this me?

In my dreams, I always steeped in the sun like a rattlesnake, tanning, mutating my DNA like a Darwinian wish, staring directly into the eye of an eclipse. My soul fluoresced, I was two sunny side up eggs cooking on the hot asphalt road in the middle of a Texas August, I refracted into a rainbow on your bedroom wall, splaying my white light, bent, I was every plant powerhouse photosynthesizing, phosphorus, Lazarus, with enough solar masses to hold the earth closer to me than the sun ever would.

As a human, my skin would always fail me, I needed to be something beyond. This is where my campfire fantasies came in, it wasn't hard for a ten year old to figure out. With self-immolation, at least my friends and parents can gather around me, tell stories and roast marshmallows. Lighting yourself on fire feels a bit like bees stinging you, if those bees were mini atom bombs going off on your skin. Once you burn thought the skin and the nerves, you no longer feel anything. Your body is the final disguise for you soul.

I mourned the loss of my life and childhood in every mea-surable unit I could comprehend at the time. I counted it in glow in the dark stars on my ceiling, in lightening bugs inside mason jars, in the days left during summer break, in moonrises, in the amount of times my head rested on a pillow with a tooth underneath, supernumerary, supernature, and most finally, in the inches of my florescent soul editing my new future, no longer holding the darkness like a shroud.

What will I be this time? If I am the birthday balloon, deflate me in front of the child, the one with the pointy hat screaming a sugary rainbow. And if I am a bible study, spread me in the wind, give me a name and tell them of my false perfection. Sometimes I want to be midnight on New Years Eve and make everything go backwards. The fireworks unburn, the lovers unkiss, permanently. No one dies, they just shrink back inside the womb and dissolve into a blood stream. I never was or would be.

There is a world where I am a sunbeam, a ghost stampede rushing through our universe. I will see the furnaces of creation, future lives, I will radiate through it, them, you, us, here: without a body to annex, swallowing the colors of time.

Sweet Bird of Paradox

by Rose Knows

She wasn't sure why she was so stunned when he placed his large calloused hand over her nose and mouth. Surely, he could read her eyes. Surely, her fear expressed itself. How could he betray her trust? Tears streamed down his hand, so he gave it a few more beats before he retracted. He sat up, looked at her confusingly, and said, "Hmm, interesting." She stared back at him, silently panting as tears cascaded her naked breasts.

The moment she closed her eyes, he began to suffocate her again. Halfway between passing out and regaining consciousness, the smell of chlorine suddenly flooded her mind with memories. She had been here before. Well, not here, exactly, but the images of that day resurfaced as she tried to gasp for air. She heard her mother screaming for someone to help as she sank to the bottom of the YMCA pool.

He examined her frightened eyes and pulled away his heavy hand. She begged for air as he sat there quixotically wondering where she was going in her head. She cried, searching his eyes for some sort of compassion. Wasn't he a professional? Didn't this make sense to him? She began to fade in and out to the pounding of each solitary tear. A distant male voice flooded her eardrums, along with the sound of heart compressions thumping endlessly. He sat there watching her and began spitting in her face, in what seemed to be the exact rhythm of her heart.

He wiped away the spit from her face and gently

placed his hand back over her nose and mouth. Slowly, he made his way down to her dripping wet cunt. Her heartrate slowed, she closed her eyes and relaxed as he skillfully ate her pussy. All the while, his hand was over her face, she had almost forgotten the need to breathe. She was irrevocably docile in this moment. Images of the pool and the piercing sound of compressions gently disintegrated as she flooded his face with her saccharine release. He removed his hand and she gingerly drank in the air. Without uttering a single word, he wiped his mouth and left.

Learned Behavior

by Krystall Schott

DONT TRUST THE
CHILDREN
THEY`VE
BEEN LISTENING TO
THE ADULTS

it REALLY THAT
SUCKS WAS
THIS a

You Have To Know
Pain
To Know Joy

by Crow Jane

THE SHRIEKING GARDEN

Born into the world,
without a choice from the first breath.
Uncomfortable and trying to understand.
Needing to be seen,
needing to be heard.
Looking for help and guidance.

No comprehension of life
but I had to start navigating through it.
There is no way to prepare yourself
for what is to come.
No human can protect you completely.
You're never really safe,
but you do get to have experiences
and gain knowledge.
The learning process isn't blissful.
I have learned the most through pain.

The trauma I felt
when my mother first left me
at school as a child
was the same sensation I felt
while watching her die.
How can the feeling be the same
when the experience itself is so different?
When one circumstance is so much more tragic
than the other?

The same mix of fear,
abandonment,

grief,
victimization,
etc.
Sometimes it's the abandonment of others,
Sometimes it's me abandoning myself.

Don't let trauma win.

"Although the world is full of suffering, it is full
also of the overcoming of it"
    -Helen Keller

Santa Claus Isn't Real

by Anthony Anthony

"Take your father his Christmas gift. The one you got him. Go on now. Go give it to him."

I am crying. Tears keep running down my face, and the more I try to get them to stop, the more they come.

I grasp my package, pulling it closer to my chest. I am reminded of the unmeasurable joy I felt while wrapping my father's gift. I am taking part in the ritual that was once kept secret to me, before I learned Santa Claus didn't exist, before my older brother came to my bedside shaking me until I woke up.

"He isn't real. Dad just came home from work really late."

"You're lying."

I open the car door to my mother's Mercury Sable. The vehicle is dusty brown, the hood baked with sun damage from the Adelanto sun. My brother and I would sit posing as pictures were taken of us, he would close his eyes every time the camera flashed.

Every day hotter than the last. Endless miles of desert where my father would walk with me, side by side, with slingshot in tow. Picking up empty Bud Light bottles. Peeling the labels from the front. Careful not to leave any trace.

Collecting grasshoppers, using my forefingers to grasp their little legs. My father showed me how to grab them so they wouldn't bite me with their surprisingly human-like jaws. I would shove them down the open neck of the bottles until they were all taking turns trying to jump out, back through the hole where I sent them to their mass grave. It was the only sense of control I had as a child when my life was constantly navigated by someone else. I felt as if I continued to accidentally swallow pennies that I sucked on while watching TV. I could have the winds blow it all back from my choking throat.

Papa. Papa. Mira lo que te compré.

I pleaded.

Walking side by side through that same desert where we went on our many walks, hunting for Gila monsters and coyotes and buried treasure, we found only abandoned pits full of people's trash. I trotted behind him in tow, begging him to come home. Trying to keep up with him as his eyes drifted out into the horizon, such fierce determination in his gaze as he looked out into a destination unknown. I never once saw him look back.

Yet I looked back.

It was Christmas. That last Christmas, when I awoke to the screaming down the hall. My older brother and younger sister were already there, staring back out at me as I cracked the door to our shared bedroom. I rubbed my eyes in unison with the screams of hatred occuring between my father and mother, before they exchanged slaps and blows. It was almost as if they were waiting for all of us to appear before showing us just how tired of each other they were. My father repeatedly hit my mother as she lay cowering under my sister's broken rocking horse, a horse I used to ride but no longer could as I had grown too big. The horse's cedar frame lay spiked and splintered under my mother's collapsed body as her screams burned holes into the back of my head.

I began to cry as I walked right into my parents bedroom and yanked the phone from the cradle, the same cradle I had lifted it from once before when I was wondering why our cable was shut off, when I called the number the silly men left on our front door hanging by a hook of paper.

If you want your cable back, call (760) XXX-XXXX

This time, I called the cops. I told them everyone in my house was crying, and we were all scared. I told them I didn't know why but my daddy wouldn't stopping hitting my mommy. I told them I needed someone to help because he wouldn't stop doing it and I just wanted to go back to sleep.

It seems like Christmas has always been a much happier time for everyone else. Every time I hear a Christmas song I can't help but be reminded of that Christmas when my dad wouldn't stop hitting my mom. He was still hitting her when the police arrived. They took my daddy away in handcuffs. I ran after him, crying, only to be picked up by a police officer, my feet kicking as I pleaded to let me go.

Let me go.

***

I hold the gift up to my dad as I am running to catch up to him. My mother has the car parked, waiting to show me that my father is leaving me and never coming back. She had warned me before he went to prison for hitting her, before I called the police.

"Keep it son. Just keep it."

My father, my father…is walking away from me, and he just keeps walking. Never stopping, never looking back at me or my siblings. I stop chasing him and I can't stop crying. He is looking forward. Looking forward as I look back and I never stop wondering where or who I should turn to. Eventually, I give up and sit down, tears falling onto the desert floor, my dad's gift right beside me while I watch fire-ants run back and forth over the sand as wind blows over my view of the horizon. The most depressing of sunsets. My last sunset with my father as he walks away. I wonder where he is going and if he is ever coming back.

SPLITTING

by Sourgirrrl

THE SHRIEKING GARDEN

It lingers and looms,
Demons in shadow play.
A fragile girl,
Who once felt safe.

Now I understand,
Nothing remains the same.
I've died before,
In a thousand subtle ways.

An error in my creation,
Doomed from the start.
Struck with a curse,
Where I mutilate my own heart.

I can't tell you how it started,
Something was never quite right,
Tried to vanish but it finds me every time.

I practiced death,
Clenched my fists.
The pills didn't work,
I can finally forgive.

I fetishized the bridge,
The noose,
And the train.
Anger subsided me
I focused on the pain.

THE SHRIEKING GARDEN

Gave everything away,
It serves no use for me.
The place that I'm going,
I don't need material things.

These scars remind me of a past life,
I don't know how I made it past 25.
I feel nothing or everything at once,
A fantasy laments in memory of us.

AFFINITY FOR
MONSTERS

by Krystall Schott

My First Porno

by Rhianna Martinez Yates

This story is that of an embarrassing nature, or should I say a primal nature. And it is true, as all good stories are. We are all born with this shameful side and I have to believe, based off of my experience so far, we will forever experiment with it; we have since our beginnings and we will until we "can't any more!" Thus: SEX.

There was no denying it as a child who's parents (thank you) never stopped her from watching explicit rated R-movies. Horror had become my favorite genre. And within horror: bloody rape, forbidden fucks and taboo seduction twisted my insides in an awesome way.

I used to make my Barbies rape each other. I remember specifically using their lifeless bodies to act out the scene from Pretty Woman, where Jason Alexander forces himself on (Pretty Woman actress's name). Now, at 25, the scene doesn't do much for me, but back then I loved it.

I was one young horn-dog. Secretly, I hoped most people were.

Sex: it's the secret everyone lives out behind closed doors. Your mother, your father, your grandparents, your professors, your boss, the barista, the waitress, the valet, the judge, the pigs…they're all fucking.

I was 8 or 9 years old when my step-uncle called my cousins and my cousin's friends into the room. Their friends were hot, two older German brothers. I was a tomboy back then so I was always with the guys and made sure I was always a part of everything. The room was boring, twin mattresses on the floor, closet, computer, desk, chair, nothing on the white smudged walls but a big window, shit blinds, whatever. This uncle was the cool step-uncle, always high energy; I guess he had a secret to show us this day. I just remember us all gathering around the computer monitor, criss cross apple sauce. He clicks a link on a website. It's an anime porn of a big spot-eyed dog licking a Japanese girl's pussy on the top of the hill outside. The frame kept switching back from her face to the dog's. Then, another link. A girl tied up and a tentacle monster ramming it's seemingly neverending tentacles into her openings.

I certainly can not blame my overactive sexual appetite on that day. It was already alive and well before then. I wasn't scared or violated or forced to do something I did not want to do. I can't help but look back and think about some of the Freudian principles that took place in my tiny little brain on that odd day. I was around five males, whom were all older than myself, and we were watching porn openly together. Though it was my first time seeing anything like that, I was acting as if it wasn't. Did this experience lead to me having a more open and accepting sexuality? Did it mold me into being more comfortable with men who act older or are, in fact, older than me? Did it help my freak fly? Was I always destined to be this sexual creature? Did I become this or was I always this?

Without sex, we would cease to exist. Is it really such a distasteful thing if it is almost completely accepted by the masses, Liberal or Republican? Even indigenous tribes are fucking. The birds and the bees.

Was I a bad child…or, am I just human?

Preschool Review

by Ryan A.R. Montez

THE SHRIEKING GARDEN

My parents found out I was going to be a boy during the ultrasound screening, as I floated in that warm darkness. My shlong was visible on the ultrasound tele. I was definitely a man. Tallywacker and all. Yes, this story is starting off with penis tone, for it is a story about penis, about mine!

I was cut out of my mama's womb like Caesar. Lived in San Gabriel, a small town on the east end of Los Angeles. Grew up in a big house, had a dog, tons o' toys, normal life for a little boy. I remember... not much. School, I remember though.

It must have been my first year of preschool. I was a naughty one, they said. Always with the dunce cap, time out boy. How can a precious boy of infinite possibility be bad? Naughty enough to be kicked out of class into the cold, and even worse...? Those low, prudish, fuckin' Catholic wenches of humanity that's how.

Here's what went down. I would get random erections in class (everywhere actually, I remember it happening a lot in parking lots) which, to me, is symbolic of being a perfectly aligned human with the chakras, working Kundalini, magick, life-force, all that jazz! I would tell the other preschoolers, "Hey I have a penus, do U?" The dude's usually got it, we'd usually laugh about it. I probably creeped some kids out, but when it came to Miss Erma Ugly Face and her cretin kid-watchers, they'd hear me and they'd rev up the torture chamber. They would hold me down, the four-year-old weirdo kid talking about his dingle, and pour the cold soap slime down my esophagus, "Bad boy!" A poor and wretched person's repressive style of discipline. I would have preferred getting the belt. The soap wouldn't clean my "dirty, non-protestant" mouth and mind.

I love my prick and always will. Why shouldn't I? The subtle power of the erection and the gentle trickling of urination is always a constant well of inspiration.

The chili powder was worse than the soap. A single tear would drip down my courageous, martyred face as my young tastebuds would smelter.

For years after this traumatic tyranny I hated flavorful foods. Anything from pasta to hamburgers I would eat plain, no condiments, no sauce. The fear and oppression of that slave god religious attitude of the preschool wenches had found it's ugly vampiric teeth clinging to the very depth of my soul, sucked. I didn't like brushing my teeth either, the soap-scum never left the palate.

Now I'm different alright. Got a chippy shoulder y'hear? Yeah, I brush my darned teeth now. Yeah, I got over my fear of flavor.

So, here's my review of this crap private school...

OMS: One Motherfuckin' Star. See you in hell fuckers.

Corridor 6

by Bobby Double

They say "the first cut is the deepest" but mine happened while slicing a tomato with a butter knife, and it didn't even bleed.

My family drove in circles around the airport for what felt like an eternity. My grandparents were coming to town for my aunt's wedding and crashing at our place. I guess they forgot to tell my parents that their flight was delayed. When finally they appeared, grandma and grandpa were to squish into the backseat with my sister and I. My sister got out to let them in. Grandpa came in first and immediately upon pressing his thigh into mine let out a very wet sounding fart which I could feel rumble through us.

"Whoops," he said, and chuckled.

I was 6 years old and had just begun appreciating mirrors in more of an adult manner. It had only been a few weeks since I started checking to see if I liked the way my hair or outfit looked on a semi-regular basis. I was especially excited for my aunt's wedding that day considering my parents had rented me my very first suit. Having never been dressed in a suit before, I couldn't wait to put it on and get a good look at myself in the mirror.

With the exception of the tie and the buttoning of my sleeves, I managed to get into the suit in a manner that I perceived to be proper and near complete. A surge of eagerness rushed through me as I burst out of my bedroom and towards the nearest bathroom to get a good look at myself.

As I rushed through the half-open bathroom door,

my mother sat on the toilet before me, a scrunched expression on her face as a loud plopping sound became audible in the toilet water beneath her.

"Mom! Why don't you ever close the door when you go?"

I rushed out of there and slammed the door behind me.

There was another bathroom upstairs – I'll head there, I thought. Running full speed, as I did a great quantity of the time, I ran into a little obstacle on the way up the stairs: grandpa. I physically ran right into him, my face to his butt, and as I did, another syrupy fart escaped.

"Whoops," he said, and chuckled.

I took a few steps back and waited for him to make his way up the stairs, and out of my way, then shot up towards the other bathroom.

Through another half open door, my father stood before me with his elephant-sized dongus pointed at the toilet bowl. A piss stream shot out with the strength of a firehose, simultaneously confusing and impressing me.

"Almost ready to go, son?"

"Yeah," I mumbled.

I peered down into the toilet bowl and watched as the astonishing force blasted the yellow waters, the surface fully covered in an array of bubbles.

"Dad, how do you make so many bubbles?"

"What?"

He chuckled as I slowly backed out of the room. I could still hear his colossal piss stream as I headed back towards the stairs, until the sound of nearby giggles distracted me.

My sister, who was 2 years my senior, was in her room with one of her girl-friends from the neighborhood. Her door was left open a crack. I peeked in and saw that they were in her bed, completely hidden under the covers. There was rapid movement and they were both giggling continuously.

I wondered, what the heck are they doing in there?

Whatever it was, it made me feel uncomfortable.

Maybe Mom is done by now, I thought, and headed back downstairs to check.

Again, a half open door presented itself, the light still on beyond it. I could hear running water coming from the bathtub inside, and assumed she must have left it filling after exiting the room. However, I was wrong, and upon opening the door I was assaulted with the vision of her in no pants, squatting and scrubbing her crotch to wash it under the faucet's running waters.

"Mom! Why? Close the door!"

I slammed the door behind me and rushed towards my parents' bedroom. The only other mirror in the house was a full length one on the back of their door. The door to their room was closed but they were both using the bathrooms so I knew they wouldn't be in there.

In a frenzy, I opened the door, plowed through, placed myself on the opposite side, and closed it again. There was a brief moment of silence as I lifted my head to finally get a good look at myself in the mirror, and just as I began to process what I saw, an outraged voice spoke up from within the room,

"Excuse me!"

As I turned towards the voice, my grandma turned to face me, head on. She stood in the center of the room with her fists balled and placed on her hips, fully nude. She appeared highly offended, though I was the one who would have her drooping, grotesque body etched into the frontlines of my mind for the rest of my life. This was my "Room 237."

Back in the hallway, I stood still as my stomach sank and Dad appeared.

"You need help with your tie, bud?"

"Yeah," I mumbled.

The wedding went off without a hitch but Mom probably shouldn't have eaten so much of that second helping of meatloaf and egg salad right before we headed home, considering that she'd also had multiple Colorado Bulldogs and always had an extremely sensitive stomach. I was crammed between her and the car door, while the rest of the backseat was filled out by my grandma and my sister, on the car ride back. We had just entered a long stretch of freeway in which there were no exits for a solid 15 minutes when Mom started squirming and cooing. The rest of the car tried to be supportive, assuring her she would make it. After five minutes of her jiggling slowly increased in intensity, I felt a little earthquake jolt from her thigh through mine and then she stopped moving entirely. I think a part of my soul died in that moment and then, from the passenger seat up front, grandpa let out another one of his juicy, signature farts.

"Whoops," he said, and chuckled.

I wanted a break from the family after all that so I asked if I could stay with my cousin of the same age, Spitzwick, for the rest of the weekend. There, it felt like we could do whatever we wanted, with no obstacles standing in our way.

At the end of the night, we crawled into his bed, threw the sheets over our heads, and discovered we shared a mutual curiosity regarding what would happen if we rubbed our nether parts together. The only thing that happened was it tickled quite a bit, which led us both to giggle vigorously. Then, an upset voice chimed in.

"What the hell are you two doing in there?"

We paused for a moment to glance over at Spitzwick's dad, Uncle Duncan, through the doorway to his room. He was sitting up in his bed looking at us very concernedly. We said nothing and carried on with what we were doing.

"Hey!"

Suddenly, something in the next room exploded and we felt the impact against our faces. When I opened my eyes, I saw blood and small fragments of what appeared to be flesh and bone scattered all over Spitzwick's face, the walls, and the bedsheets surrounding us. When I looked over to Duncan, his body was still erect but his head was missing and in it's place was a blaring golden light bursting up from inside him, to the ceiling, flooding the visible majority of the room. Spitzwick and I took each other's hands and walked towards the light.

A scattered pile of Club magazines formed a stair-case for us to make our way up onto Duncan's abnormally elevated king size bed. In synchrony, we peaked down into the hole in which the light came from, felt it envelope us entirely, then crawled in.

W.o.w.

by Chad Fjerstad

About The Artists

Jenni Zeller is a multi-media graphic designer and art director for the Los Angeles film and music industry currently living in Tijuana, Mexico. Her illustration technique is inspired by her own reflection of human cognition and problem-solving. By exhibiting strong endurance and instinctive responses, she can be easily absorbed emotionally. She has developed an inner world that is so alive, and through art, her mind expresses authentically what's going on inside. As to avoid getting caught in her own reticence, she surrenders to irrationality, absurdity, and mystery to cultivate trust within her consciousness.

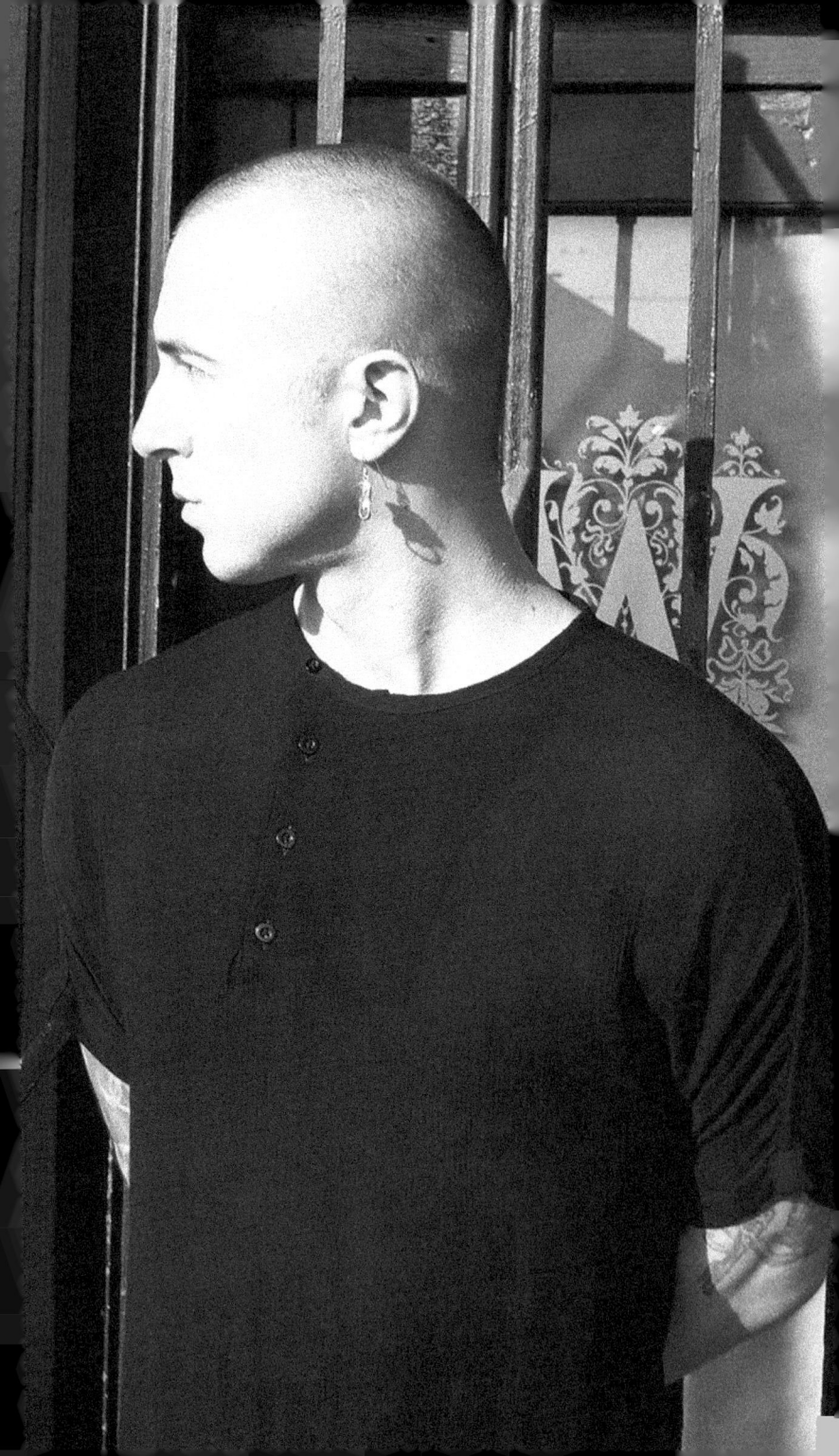

Chad Fjerstad is a multi-disciplinary artist and adult film actor living in Los Angeles. He operates the multimedia production house Ephemerol Night Terrors through which he releases all of his books and a great quantity of his music. He has released two novels: Warship Satan, and Popping Cherries.

Photo by Ruled By The Sun

The sentient cement is ready to be forged in hate and utilized in love, correcting the possession of human spirit as being acceptable behavior.

-LaBanna Babalon

Kris Kidd is an LA-based model, poet and confessional essayist. He is the author of *I Can't Feel My Face* (2014), *Down for Whatever* (2016), and the writer behind *#ELSEWHERE,* a "clinically depressed sex column" for Nakid Magazine.

Photo by Ben Cope

Born and raised in California, **Krystall Schott** grew up in the suburbs and had a nice, normal(ish) childhood, although she was probably largely shaped by being born into a horse girl lifestyle, having parrot head parents and a near death toadstool experience at the age of 3. Being a very awkward teenager with no real close friends, she was somehow drafted into modeling at age 16 and enjoyed it mostly because she got to pretend she was a secret agent. Though, no one really hired her for anything. Maybe it was due to her ridiculously large foot size, bizarre fashion sense, or disdain for the fact that she was supposed to be a girl, she doesn't know.

At 18, she went to New York and really killed it in the awkward category, as well as becoming a much more successful secret agent. It was around this time that she was gifted a $1 watercolor set (the best gift she ever received) from her new best friend, which sent her back into doing the thing that she loved most. She'd been failing to keep up since being so distracted by being a secret agent: making a mess.

Since then her mess has grown into many mediums and is ever growing. She cannot stop creating and hopes someday it will save the world, which has always been her main goal, even in being a secret agent.

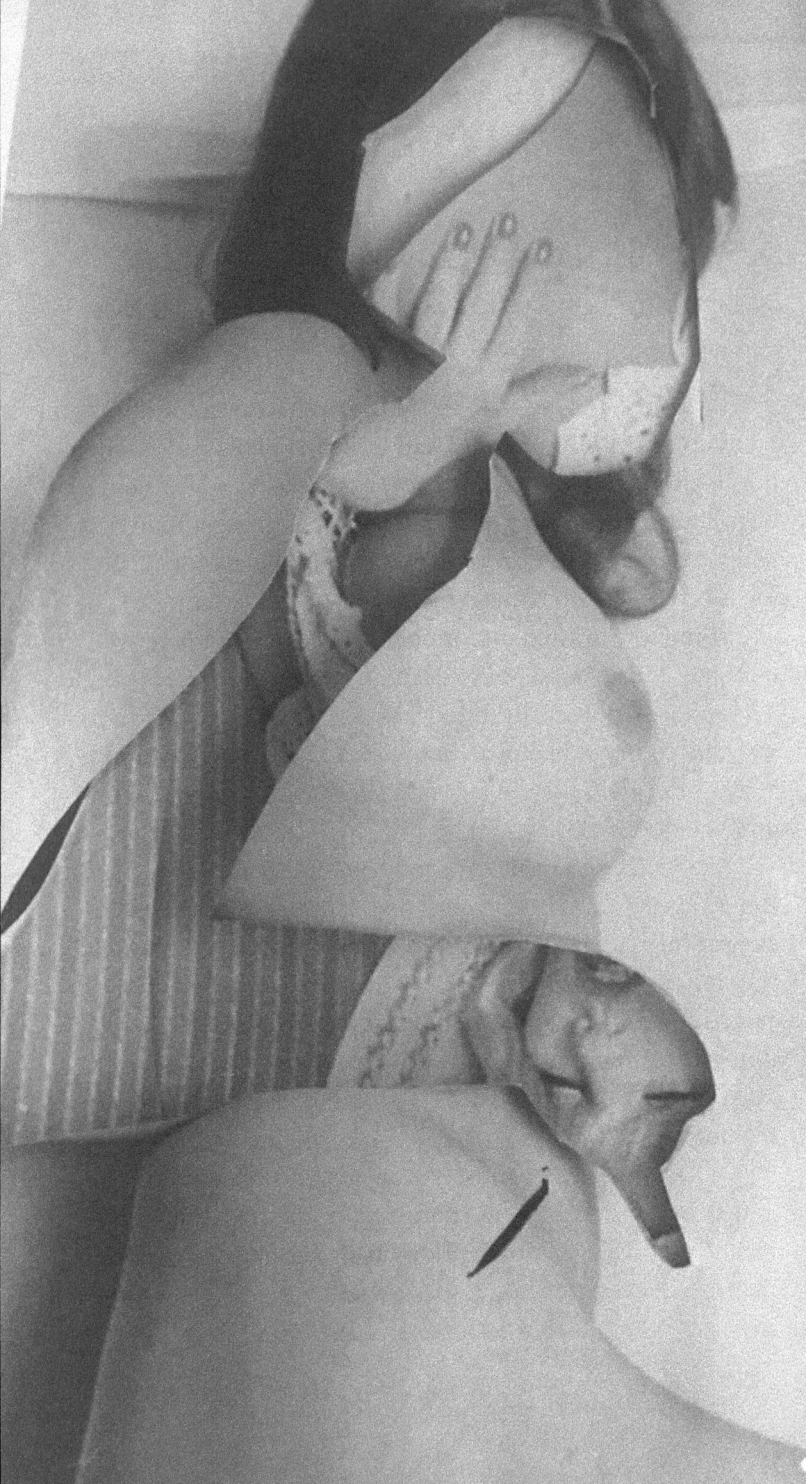

Allessandra Tipacti

I wrote 'Shit Starter' in explanation of a particular re occurring frustration I have had throughout my life. In it, there is a catharsis to finally outline (though brief) this particular dichotomy. Like a confession, a space to state my point of view as opposed to always having to think or speak of it in some ramble. There is a theme of extreme opposites, a position of power and the position of being helpless; in a world where for whatever reason you might find yourself under a microscope, the need to just be and how hard that balance is to come across. There is a theme of violence and a hope for peace.

Hether Fortune is a musician, poet, writer, and artist from Oakland, California. She fronted the band Wax Idols for a decade and is currently at work on a debut solo album as well as a memoir. She published her first book of poetry, Waiting in Various Lines (2013-2017), earlier this year.

Phoenix Askani is a model and writer living in Los Angeles. She is also co-host of the Sex Magic podcast.

Photo by Steve Agee

Actually Huizenga is an underground filmmaker and musician from Los Angeles. She has a band called Patriarchy.

Véro Anease is a silversmith - her work can be found at vspiria.com

Living with partially paralyzed vocal cords, she's learned that speaking quietly forces everyone to listen to her with more intent. However, she feels that verbal communication is incredibly limiting. So, she prefers to express herself in any other form than talking, whenever possible.

Christopher Zeischegg is the author of three books: Come to my Brother, The Wolves That Live in Skin and Space, and Body to Job. He lives in Los Angeles.

Meaghan O'Keefe is an artist and comic book illustrator in Los Angeles, CA.

Josh Beck

Raised by feral lesbians & drag queens in the
streets of Portland, Oregon - as a child he was kidnapped
by Shanghai slave traders & forced into fighting pits. He
never learned how to read or write & spoke only in primi-
tive grunts & screams. It wasn't until a traveling merchant
discovered him that he was rescued & returned to the
United States to find sanctuary in Los Angeles. A journal-
ist at heart.

Niko Sonnberger is 60% H2O, 40% filmmaker who is putting the "try" back into "poetry".

There's always some Rose, somewhere, with a big nose who Knows.

Rose Knows is a native Los Angelina, DJ, amateur writer, True Crime Trivia Maitresse, Provocateur and Jill of all trades. She enjoys dark films in sunny places, creating magick, contemplating the absurdity of reality and the desperate need for art that provokes. You can follow her musings at @rose.knows and her writing at @eyesthatwhisper

L.A. based artist, musician, and activist, **Crow Jane.** Known for playing guitar in the art punk band Egrets on Ergot, doing vocals in the No Wave band Prissy Whip, and taking part in playing characters/singing in the Dangerhouse 77' band The Deadbeats. Her current art medium outside of music is makeup and makeup FX for film around the Los Angeles area.

Photo by David Fearn

Anthony Anthony encapsulates what he considers an abnormality in a compromised system of conjoined parts. He establishes a new indefinite narrative of living unpossessed by absences of people in his past. He lives with his cat, Piccolo, and snake, Lady Babalon. He also enjoys driving to local state parks and is currently enrolled to earn a California Optician's License.

Sourgirrrl is an artist from San Francisco, CA. She received her bachelors degree in Fine Art at Laguna College of Art and Design. She works primarily with watercolors and gouache. Her curiosity about the world and how we process emotions is what drives her. She gravitates towards the darker parts of her mind and tries to emulate those emotions.

Photo by Nedda Afsari

Rhianna Martinez Yates

I'm a third generation chicana, California born and raised. My Mexican grandfather Dr. Ralph Martinez helped design the internet, he was head dean of the science departments at USD UTEP UofA, he worked at the pentagon and also has legit been to Area 51. Everything I do is for him. RIP. I have this sort of a secret, something a lot of people don't know about me, I used to be addicted to meth. I'm 6 years clean. I plan to someday share my horror story with everyone and I hope I can help someone a long the way. People know me from instagram @skuzishrugish - I used to do makeup and styling for a porn company. I've been spotted at porn events and even in a No Jumper interview. I'm also a retired ********** at 25. Chase the bag long enough and you will catch up to it. Currently I'm in school for fashion design, I do styling on the side, and recently have been on an entrepreneur adventure, investing in new ways. I am blessed to be a millennial. I also paint. I've been experimenting with impressionism. Follow my art page @ millenialximpressionist - I used to be in a punk band. I was the hot girl puking blood on stage in a chaotic possession. We were called katemo$$. I left because we never made any money, but we did manage to tour europe for a month with our friends ho99o9. you should look us up next time you have a nice sit with the family. Be on the look out for my up and coming clothing brand MarteMone. AND REMEMBER LOVES: DONT FUCK RAW! UNLESS YOU'RE BOTH TESTED! ALWAYS PAY HOMAGE WHEN ITS DUE. AND...
GOING TO COLLEGE IS SEXY!

Do what thou wilt shall be the whole of the Law. **Ryan A.R - Montez** is a Thelemite from the Valley of Los Angeles. He spins records around the L.A. area and has special plans for this world. His hobbies include Ceremonial Magick and Rock n Roll. This is his first time being published. Love is the law, love under will.

EPHEMEROL
= NIGHT =
TERRORS

© 2019

www.ingramcontent.com/pod-product-compliance
Lightning Source LLC
Chambersburg PA
CBHW060207070426
42447CB00035B/2802